TECHNOLOGY IN
ANCIENT CHINA

CHARLIE SAMUELS

Gareth Stevens
Publishing

Please visit our website, www.garethstevens.com. For a free color catalog of all our high-quality books, call toll-free 1-800-542-2595 or fax 1-877-542-2596.

Library of Congress Cataloging-in-Publication Data

Samuels, Charlie.
Technology in ancient China / by Charlie Samuels.
   p. cm. — (Technology in the ancient world)
Includes index.
ISBN 978-1-4339-9625-2 (pbk.)
ISBN 978-1-4339-9626-9 (6-pack)
ISBN 978-1-4339-9624-5 (library binding)
1. Technology—China--History—To 1500—Juvenile literature. 2. Technological innovations—China—History—To 1500—Juvenile literature. 3. China—Civilization—To 221 B.C—Juvenile literature. I. Samuels, Charlie, 1961-. II. Title.
T16.S25 2014
931—dc23

Published in 2014 by
Gareth Stevens Publishing
111 East 14th Street, Suite 349
New York, NY 10003

For Brown Bear Books Ltd:
Editorial Director: Lindsey Lowe
Managing Editor: Tim Cooke
Children's Publisher: Anne O'Daly
Art Director: Jeni Child
Designer: Lynne Lennon
Picture Manager: Sophie Mortimer

Picture Credits
Front Cover: Shutterstock: Hung Chung Chih

Alamy: blickwinkel 43; **Public Domain:** 11, 21; **Shutterstock:** 17, 28, 20, 34, 35, 40, Antonio Abrignani 32, Venus Angel 5, Robert Anthony 27, Norman Chan 31, Hung Chung Chih, 37, William Ju 20, Kentoch 16, Valery Shanin 6, Yanfel Sun 10, P. Witthaya 42; **Thinkstock:** Hemera 38, Ingram Publishing 36, istockphoto 1, 9, 12, 13, 14, 15, 18, 22, 24, 33, Photos.com 8, 41, Top Photo Group, 4, 26.

All artworks © Brown Bear Books Ltd

Brown Bear Books has made every attempt to contact the copyright holders. If you have any information please contact smortimer@windmillbooks.co.uk

Manufactured in the United States of America

CPSIA compliance information: Batch #CS13GS: For further information contact Gareth Stevens, New York, New York at 1-800-542-2595.

CONTENTS

INTRODUCTION

China is the world's oldest continuous civilization. It has been at the forefront of technological innovation for more than four thousand years. While their enemies were still fighting with stone clubs, soldiers of the Shang Dynasty (c.1600–1046 B.C.E.) were fighting with bronze weapons. From Roman times into the Middle Ages, Chinese technology was taken along the Silk Road to the West. The Silk Road took its name from one of China's greatest exports.

Dating in parts from the seventh century B.C.E., the Great Wall of China was one of the largest construction projects ever undertaken.

The Chinese brought the world paper and printing, gunpowder, the magnetic compass, the rudder, and a harness that transformed the use of horses in transportation and agriculture. Countless innovations were made by unknown artisans; other inventions were the result of breakthroughs by imperial officials.

A LONG HISTORY

Chinese history is divided into dynasties from 3000 B.C.E. until the end of the imperial government in the early 20th century. The northern and southern parts of the country were originally separate, but were unified by the First Emperor, Qin Shi Huangdi, in 221 B.C.E. A long series of dynasties then rose and fell in China. Some of the most important were the Tang, Song, Yuan, Ming, and Qing dynasties. This book will introduce you to the most important examples of the technology behind this remarkably long-lived civilization.

China was so famous for its high-quality pottery and porcelain that the country's name, China, is used to describe all such objects.

TECHNOLOGICAL BACKGROUND

Chinese technology usually drew on older practices from within China itself. The country was so vast and its civilization was so advanced that it tended to take little notice of other cultures.

One of the earliest Chinese dynasties to develop a significant engineering technology was the Shang (c.1600–1046 B.C.E.). The Shang built vast tombs for their rulers. They dug burial

The terracotta warriors of the First Emperor are evidence of the skills of early Chinese potters.

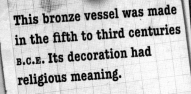

This bronze vessel was made in the fifth to third centuries B.C.E. Its decoration had religious meaning.

chambers up to 40 feet (12 m) deep. Tomb engineering would reach its peak with the magnificent tomb of the First Emperor, Qin Shi Huangdi (259–210 B.C.E.). He was buried in an underground re-creation of his capital city, complete with a river of mercury. He also ordered the construction of more than 8,000 life-sized soldiers to protect him in the next life, together with horses and chariots. The warriors were made in molds, but a layer of clay was added so that each warrior had a unique face.

METAL WORKING

The ancient Chinese were also great metal workers. The Shang used bronze to make weapons and vessels, but not for tools. The tradition of metal working continued. In the sixth century B.C.E., the Chinese became the first people in the world to cast iron.

FARMING

The Chinese were 2,200 years ahead of Europe in farming technology. While European farmers were still scattering seeds, by the sixth century B.C.E. Chinese farmers were sowing their crops in rows. They made sure their vegetable beds were well weeded. Iron hoes and the plow also helped Chinese farming further.

The Chinese improved the plow. They also introduced the practice of growing rice in flooded fields.

Farmers began planting in rows in the sixth century B.C.E. It made crops easier to weed and harvest.

In northern China, the chief crops were wheat and millet, but in the warmer south, the main crop was rice. From about 6500 B.C.E., the Chinese grew rice in waterlogged paddy fields. Paddy fields were created on large flat areas or on narrow terraces on steep mountainsides. By the first century B.C.E., farmers used a multi-tubed seed drill to speed up sowing in rows.

METAL TOOLS

Metal tools sped up farming. The iron plow appeared in the sixth century B.C.E. with a blade shaped to cut through the soil. The plow was pulled by oxen or water buffalo.

TECHNICAL SPECS

- In the sixth or fifth century B.C.E., the Chinese invented the cast-iron hoe, which made weeding easier.
- The development of the swan-neck hoe in the first century B.C.E. meant farmers could weed around plants without damaging them.
- In the first century B.C.E., the moldboard plow was invented. It turned the soil, releasing nutrients. It let farmers work less fertile soil.
- The square-pallet chain pump raised water through a series of wooden platforms (pallets) attached to a metal chain. One pump could raise water 12 feet (4 m).

WATER ENGINEERING

Chinese farmers relied on the seasonal flooding of rivers to spread nutrient-rich silt over their fields. But rivers such as the Huang He (Yellow) and Chang Jiang (Yangtze) could be a curse as well as a blessing. Floods ruined crops and killed hundreds of thousands of people. The Huang He was known as "China's Sorrow."

China's rivers frequently overflowed their banks; the worst floods drowned many thousands of people.

The Chinese tried to stop the rivers overflowing their banks. They lined the channels with articial reinforcements such as fascines or gabions to prevent erosion. Artificial earth banks called levees were also built along the rivers.

IRRIGATION PROJECT

Around 256 B.C.E, an official named Li Bing built the Dujiangyan irrigation system on the Minjang River. Its purpose was to irrigate a large area of land and to prevent the city of Chengdu flooding. It diverted river water to irrigate crops, drained sediment, and controlled the annual floods.

In the highlands, China's rivers run through gorges gathering sediment that is deposited downstream.

TECHNICAL SPECS

- Fascines and gabions prevented erosion. Fascines are bundles of brushwood tied together; gabions are baskets or cages filled with stones.
- The Dujiangyan irrigation system is still in use today.
- A barrier divided the Minjang River into two streams, called the inner and outer rivers. A spillway diverted sand and stones from the inner river to the outer river. Like the neck of a bottle, the spillway brought controlled amounts of water into the inner river.
- During the low-water season, 60 percent of the river's flow was diverted into the inner river for irrigation. In the flood season, the direction of the flow was reversed to stop flooding.

COUNTING

The abacus is still used in Chinese stores. Skilled users can make calculations at lightning speeds.

People have always needed to count and to keep a record of their counting. Early peoples gave each number its own name and character. The system was clumsy and relied on remembering many numbers. Chinese mathematicians began using the decimal system we use today.

The Chinese came up with the new system of counting in the fourth century B.C.E. It used the digits 1 to 9 and symbols for 10, 100, and 1,000. These few symbols could be combined to write any number.

RODS AND FRAMES

The Chinese invented the idea of zero. Mathematicians calculated with bars called counting rods. They left a space for a zero; later, they used a character. For sums involving larger numbers, people used the abacus, a wooden frame with columns of beads. The invention became a vital tool, not just for mathematicians, but also for astronomers and merchants.

TECHNICAL SPECS

- The Chinese use of 0 to 9 is the foundation of our decimal (meaning 10) system.
- The Chinese began using the abacus between 1000 and 500 B.C.E.
- An abacus had two decks separated by a bar. Each bead on the lower deck equaled one unit; those on the upper deck equaled five units. To count, the beads were slid toward the central bar.
- By the second century B.C.E., the Chinese used negative numbers, 100 years before Europeans. They used black rods for negative numbers and red for positive numbers.

The abacus has been in use for around 3,000 years. It counts in ones, fives, and tens.

PRINTING

The Chinese made the written word widely available. Not only did they invent paper and ink; they also invented woodblock printing and printing with movable type. This meant books could be printed in large numbers so more people could read them.

Ts'ai Lun, head of the imperial workshops, is said to have invented paper in 105 C.E. Early paper was made from rags, bamboo, mulberry bark, wheat stalks, and even rice. The fibers were separated, then soaked. A film of fibers was spread on a paper mold and left to dry. This paper was hard to write on, so people carried on writing on pottery, silk, and even turtle shells.

In movable type, symbols were carved into blocks that were assembled to make a page of text.

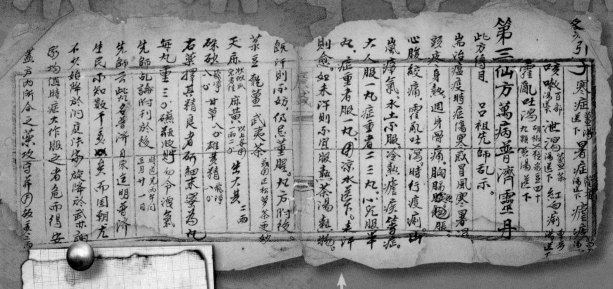

In Chinese script, characters stand for words rather than letters; there are many thousands of characters.

TECHNICAL SPECS

- The first Chinese books were made from bamboo strips, which were tied together.
- Tien Lcheu invented "Indian ink" in 2697 B.C.E. from a mix of lamp oil, soot from smoke, gelatin from donkey skin, and musk from deer.
- The first books with paper were rolled into long scrolls.
- The world's first printed book, the Diamond Sutra, was printed from woodblocks in 868.
- Blocks for movable type were carved in clay, which was fired to make it hard.
- Wood blocks for up to 80,000 different characters were needed to print a book.

PRINTING PROCESS

Printing was a slow process. A page of characters was carved onto a stone block; ink was applied and then paper was pressed against the stone. By the eighth century C.E., printers used wooden blocks that were easier to carve. In 1041, Bi Sheng created movable type. Chinese characters were each carved into a separate block. They were assembled to make a page, but could then be reused to make another page.

MONEY

Chinese money existed in various shapes for centuries before it became standard for coins to be round.

Early civilizations traded without money. They swapped goods for things they wanted, a system called bartering. The Chinese first had the idea of money: a unit that could be exchanged for any type of goods. Money made buying and selling goods much easier. It also enabled people to move their wealth from one place to another more easily.

The first metal coins appeared during the Zhou Dynasty (1046–256 B.C.E.). They were shaped as spades, knives, or shoes. These coins were heavy to use. Later coins had a hole in the center to make them lighter. They were threaded on a string or belt and worn around the waist.

PAPER MONEY

After the invention of paper and printing, paper money was introduced because it was easy to carry. Banks issued notes that could be exchanged for coins at another bank. By the Song Dynasty (960–1279 C.E.) everyone used this paper money.

Coins were cast with characters explaining their origin. This proved that they were official currency.

TECHNICAL SPECS

- The earliest money in China appeared during the Shang Dynasty (1600–1046 B.C.E.), when people traded using cowrie shells.
- The First Emperor Qin (259–210 B.C.E.) standardized money throughout the country.
- The First Emperor introduced round bronze coins, called *cash*. They were in use for 2,000 years.
- Paper money was called flying money because it often blew away.
- Coins were made from silver until the First Emperor introduced bronze coins.
- Coins were cast in molds rather than being stamped, as in Europe.

BRONZE AND METALWORKING

As early as 4000 B.C.E. the Chinese learned how to make bronze by mixing copper and tin. This, along with the invention of kilns that could heat metal ores to a high temperature, transformed China. Metal replaced wood and pottery. It was used to make farming tools, containers, decorative objects, weapons, and musical instruments.

This bronze vessel was an incense burner. Metal could be colored by a process known as lacquering.

Chinese potters developed the first kilns as ovens to fire pottery, and later to melt copper. They worked out that adding tin lowered the melting point of copper, so the kilns did not have to be so hot. This made bronze, which had several advantages over copper. It was harder, so it lasted longer. Workers cast bronze using molds. This allowed the creation of complex objects.

IRON MAKING

From about 2000 B.C.E., the Chinese used blast furnaces to extract iron. A bellows blew a stream of air into the furnace to prevent the temperature from falling. Adding phosphorus to the iron lowered its melting point from 2066 to 1742°F (1130–950°C). Europeans did not learn to cast iron until the Middle Ages.

TECHNICAL SPECS

- Changing the proportions of tin to copper created bronze in different colors and hardness.
- Iron was used in ancient China for farming tools, cast-iron pots and pans, and even toys.
- Blast furnaces existed in China almost 2,000 years before the process was discovered in Europe.
- By the fifth century B.C.E., good quality cast-iron farm tools and weapons were being produced.
- The Chinese made steel. Emperor Liu Bang (256–195 B.C.E.) was said to have owned a steel sword.

HOW TO...

Chinese craftsmen cast molten bronze in molds to make complicated shapes. The mold was made from clay. This one used 10 pieces. There was a central core and an outer case with a lid and a base. The bronze was poured in through a hole at the top and filled the space between the core and the case. When it was cool, it was taken out and the mold was reused.

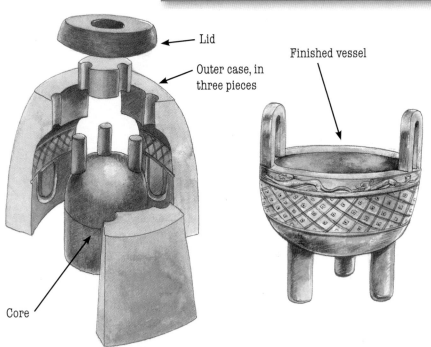

Lid

Outer case, in three pieces

Finished vessel

Core

ASTRONOMY

The Chinese believed that the heavens influenced what happened on Earth. The movement of planets and stars shaped their religion and politics. To keep the world in order, the emperor had to perform rituals according to an accurate calendar. Chinese astronomers carefully studied the skies to make sure the calendar was correct.

In 52 B.C.E., the Chinese invented an armillary sphere. It used a series of interlocked rings to measure the paths of planets and stars.

In 175 C.E. the design was improved to show the paths of the moon, planets, and sun. Astronomers could now accurately chart the sky.

This armillary sphere was made in the 17th century for the Chinese emperor.

The Chinese were among the first people to produce maps of the stars and to keep records of other things they saw in the skies.

The Chinese were among the earliest people to record the stars. They also noted events like sunspots and supernovas. In 2005 archaeologists found the remains of one of the world's oldest observatories at Linfen in Shanxi province. It dates back 4,100 years.

MEASURING TIME

In addition to astronomy, the Chinese used water clocks to measure time. The simplest water clocks used water dripping through a hole to measure the passing of time. But water clocks could also be more complicated. Su Song (1020–1101) designed an astronomical clock tower. Powered by a waterwheel, the tower was 30 feet (9 m) tall.

TECHNICAL SPECS

- The calendar was based on the moon. A year had 12 months of 29 or 30 days, starting with the new moon.
- The Chinese use a cycle of 12 animals for the years. For example, 2012 was the year of the dragon.
- The oldest Chinese mathematical text, from before 200 B.C.E., had many astronomical calculations.
- The Chinese observed sunspots as early as the fourth century B.C.E.; sunspots are cooler areas on the surface of the sun.
- An 11th-century C.E. water-driven astronomical clock mapped the stars as well as telling the time.

BUILDING

The Chinese started to live in cities from the Shang Dynasty (c. 1600–1046 B.C.E.) onward. A wall was always built around the city to protect it from invaders. Buildings were constructed from earth, timber, bricks, and tiles. The most important city was wherever the emperor lived. At first this was Xi'an, and later it was Beijing.

The buildings of Beijing's Forbidden City were laid out according to the rules of symmetry and feng shui.

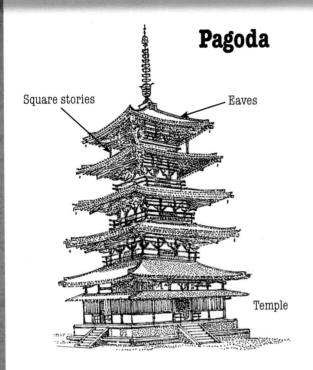

Pagoda

Square stories

Eaves

Temple

TECHNICAL SPECS

- Feng shui means "wind and water." It is based on the belief that everything is connected by an invisible force (*qi*), which must be allowed to flow at all times.
- Chinese Buddhists built pagodas. These towers were based on the shape of monuments in India, the homeland of Buddhism.
- Chinese pagodas had many stories, each marked by roof eaves. A wooden pagoda built soon after 600 C.E. at Chang'an was 330 feet (100 m) tall.
- The Forbidden City in Beijing was begun in 1406; the city within a city had more than 800 buildings for the imperial government.

Cities and homes were built upon the same strict patterns. These were based on the rules of symmetry. Homes lined up on a north–south axis. They were built according to the rules of feng shui, which aims to harmonize the home by clearing the paths of invisible energy forces all around us.

BUILDING TECHNIQUES

Houses were built from earth packed inside a wooden frame. Once the wall was complete, the wooden frame was removed. Earth bricks were also used. In a palace, the bricks might weigh up to 110 pounds (50 kg). Roofs were made from earthenware tiles resting on a wooden frame.

THE GREAT WALL

The Great Wall followed the shape of the landscape. Watchtowers were built at regular intervals to house soldiers on guard.

The Great Wall was one of history's largest construction projects. The first sections date from the seventh century B.C.E., when rival states built walls for defense. In 215 B.C.E. the First Emperor (259–210 B.C.E.) ordered the walls to be joined together. After 10 years' work, the completed wall ran 5,500 miles (8,850 km) along China's border.

The earliest sections of the wall were built from compacted earth mixed with stones and twigs. Later, bricks were used. Brick-making workshops were set up along the wall.

LATER CONSTRUCTION

During the Ming dynasty (1368–1644), the wall was rebuilt in stone. Square towers with battlements were built at regular intervals from which soldiers kept watch. They signaled from one tower to another with flags, fires, and drums. Along the top of the wall was a 12-foot (4 m) wide walkway for marching soldiers.

TECHNICAL SPECS

- The bottom of the wall was about 21 feet 4 inches (6.5 m) wide; the top was 19 feet (5.8 m) wide and carried a 12-foot (4 m) walkway.
- The average height of the wall was 23–26 feet (7–8 m).
- Gateways jutted out from the wall at important intersections on trade routes. These fortified, 30-feet (10 m) tall gateways allowed people to pass through the wall. To keep them secure, they had double wooden doors with heavy metal bolts.
- The original workforce on the wall were criminals and farmers. Conditions were harsh. It was said that a worker died for every 5 feet (1.5 m) of completed wall.

Building the wall

The earliest sections of the wall joined together existing defenses on China's northern border. They were made from compacted earth or from mud bricks; brick-making kilns were built at regular intervals along the wall. There were watchtowers along the whole length of the wall.

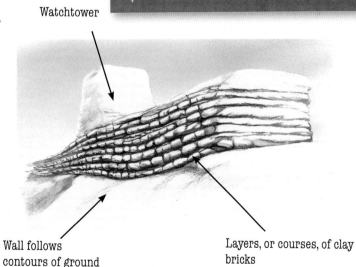

Watchtower

Wall follows contours of ground

Layers, or courses, of clay bricks

TRANSPORTATION

The First Emperor (221–210 B.C.E.) unified his vast empire by building roads and canals. He built a 4,350-mile (7,000 km) road to connect his capital, Xianyang, with the furthest parts of the empire. By the end of the second century B.C.E., China had 22,000 miles (35,400 km) of roads.

China's paved roads were all built to a standard width to make it easier for vehicles to travel around.

Metal stirrups made riding and longer journeys easier.

Travelers went on foot, on horseback, or in horse-drawn carts and carriages. All roads were the same width and all carts were the same size, so they could travel on any road. The roads were paved with stone and lined with trees.

HARNESSING HORSE POWER

The invention of the horse harness in the fifth century B.C.E. transformed transportation. The harness allowed horses to pull heavier loads. The biggest improvement for riders was the metal stirrup. Cloth stirrups were probably used by nomads such as the Mongols. The Chinese invented iron and bronze stirrups in the third century C.E.

TECHNICAL SPECS

- Chinese carts had two large wheels and silk covers to keep off the sun or the rain.
- The breastcollar harness invented by the second century B.C.E. allowed horses to use all their strength for pulling. It appeared in Europe over 1,000 years later.
- Stirrups gave riders stability, so they could ride for longer and further.
- Chinese travelers used maps to find their way around.
- Chinese maps put south at the top and north at the bottom.
- Chinese maps were the first to use grids and coordinates.

GRAND CANAL

The Grand Canal and its linked waterways joined a huge region of China together for the first time.

China's great rivers, such as the Huang He (Yellow) and Chang Jiang (Yangtze), run mainly from west to east. The Chinese built canals to make it possible to travel virtually everywhere by water. Water travel was safer and faster than road travel. It was also the best way to transport heavy goods, such as grain.

As early as the eighth century B.C.E., the Chinese built waterways for irrigation. The first transportation canal was dug in the sixth or fifth century B.C.E. It connected the Huang He and Huai rivers.

GRAND CANAL

The Grand Canal was completed in the seventh century C.E. It was really a series of waterways that linked six river systems. It made it possible to travel by water from Hangzhou in the south to Beijing in the north. The canal is still in use today.

TECHNICAL SPECS

- The Grand Canal was the longest water system of the ancient world: 1,100 miles (1,770 km).
- As many as five million laborers worked on the construction of the Grand Canal.
- In 984 C.E. Assistant Transport Commissioner Qiao Weiyo invented the pound lock. This allowed barges to climb or descend in elevation with ease.
- In the mid-15th century, the government used 11,775 barges to move grain along the Grand Canal to China's cities; more than 121,500 soldiers worked on the grain boats.

HOW TO...

The pound lock had two sets of gates that shut with the boat between them. Sluice gates could then be opened in the upper or lower gate to allow the water level inside the lock to be raised or lowered. The next gate was then opened so that the boat could continue along the canal. Before the lock was invented, boats had to be raised or lowered between canals using ropes, which took a long time and was very dangerous.

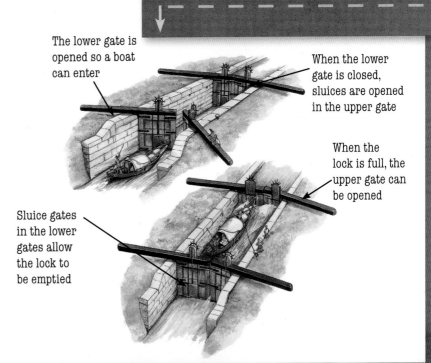

The lower gate is opened so a boat can enter

When the lower gate is closed, sluices are opened in the upper gate

When the lock is full, the upper gate can be opened

Sluice gates in the lower gates allow the lock to be emptied

MARINE TRANSPORTATION

This model shows a Chinese compass with a magnetized spoon. The spoon's handle always pointed to the south.

The Chinese were great sailors. They used new types of ships, such as the junk. They also invented the rudder to steer vessels, and bulkheads which made hulls stronger. And to navigate at sea, they invented the first magnetic compass.

Chinese scientists learned about the magnetism of Earth about 2000 B.C.E. They also knew that a magnetic stone always turned north–south. They used such stones, called lodestones, to plot a course or to steer in the dark.

The junk appeared during the Han Dynasty (206 B.C.E.–220 C.E.). Its flat bottom and raised stern (back) made it stable and good for carrying cargo. Its square sails were made from matting and divided into sections by wooden poles, known as battens. This allowed the sails to be partly raised or lowered. The rudder at the stern steered the boat by changing the flow of water past the hull. Bulkheads were small watertight compartments in the junk's hull. They prevented the boat sinking if it became holed. Such technological advances made the junk and other vessels very reliable in open seas.

TECHNICAL SPECS

- The Chinese made the first compass with dials and pointers by rubbing a metal needle on a lodestone to make it magnetic.
- The rudder dates from the second century C.E. Previously sailors had used large oars to steer their ships. The rudder meant ships could be far larger. China's navy became the biggest in the world.
- Junk sails were made from natural fibers such as grass or bamboo.
- The Chinese invented paddle boats in the fifth century C.E. The boats were powered by men walking on treadmills to turn waterwheels on the sides of the vessel.

The junk is still in daily use in China. This is a tourist vessel, but junks are also used for transporting cargo.

EVERYDAY INVENTIONS

The wheelbarrow could carry heavy loads. The long handles acted as levers and made the wheelbarrow easier to push.

Some Chinese inventions have been in continuous use for centuries. Their design has never needed improvement. They include the wheelbarrow, the umbrella, and the kite. Equipment for sports such as badminton also originated in ancient China.

The umbrella was invented in China up to 4,000 years ago. The first parasols were used to keep off the sun, rather than the rain. It was only later that parasols were waterproofed.

THE WOODEN OX

It is not known when the wheelbarrow was invented, but it appears in tomb paintings from the first century C.E. The large handcart was nicknamed the "wooden ox." They were used to transport everything, including people. Some versions had a front wheel; others had a central wheel.

TECHNICAL SPECS

- Wax and lacquer were used to waterproof paper parasols.
- The collapsible umbrella was in use by 21 C.E.
- Central–wheel handcarts could carry up to six people. The longer the handles, the less force needed to move the wheelbarrow. Some wheelbarrows were even fitted with sails.
- The first kites appeared some 2,800 years ago. They were bamboo frames covered with paper or silk.
- The earliest use of kites was military. Kites were used to distract the enemy and to send messages over long distances.

The first umbrellas were parasols made from paper. The paper was later covered with wax or laquer to make it waterproof.

MEDICINE

The ancient Chinese believed that eveything in the world had two opposing qualities: yin (female) and yang (male). A sickness in the body was a sign that the yin and yang harmony was out of balance. The purpose of Chinese medicine was to restore that balance. Doctors used a variety of techniques. Acupuncture and herbal remedies are still used today, not only in China but also around the world.

Traditional Chinese medicine is popular in many parts of the world. It is based on herbs and minerals specially mixed for each patient.

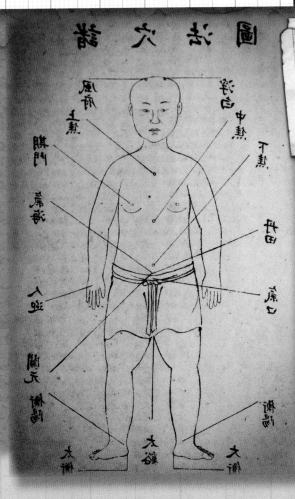

This early acupuncture diagram shows the needle insertion points to cure a particular condition.

TECHNICAL SPECS

- Some Chinese remedies used body parts from animals. There is still an illegal market for body parts from endangered species, such as tigers and rhinos.
- Male doctors were not allowed to touch female patients. Dolls were used to explain diagnoses.
- Acupuncture first appeared around 2,700 B.C.E.
- In the 16th century C.E., Doctor Li Shizhen listed 1,892 herbs and 11,000 prescriptions in a book titled *Bencao Gangmu*.

MEDICAL PRACTICE

Acupuncture works on the principle that the life force is contained in 12 lines (meridians) that link parts of the body. If a person becomes sick, a meridian is blocked. A tiny needle is inserted into the skin to unblock the meridian. Herbal, mineral, and animal remedies are even older than the use of acupuncture. Remedies are often taken in tea. Every remedy is made up for the individual, so no two remedies are the same. Many remedies, such as taking wormwood for fevers, are still used today.

SILK MAKING

Making silk was one of the greatest Chinese discoveries. The Chinese thought silk was a gift from the gods. For thousands of years, emperors kept its production secret from the outside world. Trading silk along the Silk Road to the West made China very wealthy.

Silk comes from the cocoon of the silk moth. The caterpillar spins a cocoon around its body while it changes into an adult. When the cocoon is put into boiling water, the thread of the cocoon loosens. The long threads are twisted together to make a yarn used in weaving.

The fibers surrounding the cocoon of the silk moth can be pulled into a single filament several yards long.

LONG HISTORY

Experts believe that the Chinese were weaving silk as early as 3000 B.C.E. The fabric has many advantages. It is light but strong, and is cool in the summer and warm in the winter. For centuries the cloth was so highly valued that only the emperor, his family, and the highest-ranking nobles were allowed to wear silk. Later the use of silk became more widespread. It was used for paintings, wall hangings, and decorations. Important documents were written on silk.

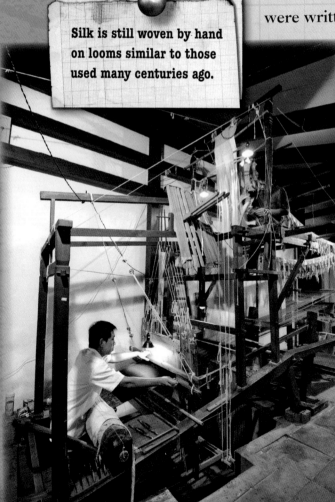

Silk is still woven by hand on looms similar to those used many centuries ago.

TECHNICAL SPECS

- The silkworm increases almost 10,000 times in weight before it starts to spin its cocoon.
- A single silk moth lays 200–300 eggs at a time that hatch into silkworms.
- A cocoon can produce a thread up to 3,000 feet (915 m) long.
- It takes thousands of cocoons to make 3 feet (1 m) of cloth.
- Silk is so strong it was used for strings in ancient musical instruments.
- The Silk Road got its name because silk was the most valuable cargo traded from China to the West.

WEAPONS AND WARFARE

For long periods of history, China was dominated by warlords who created their own private armies.

For centuries, rival Chinese dynasties fought wars to try to gain power. Weapons technology improved greatly. The invention of the crossbow gave even unskilled archers the ability to kill people from long range. Although the ancient Chinese knew about gunpowder, they rarely used it for weapons.

INTO BATTLE

China's warlords gathered armies of armored infantry, cavalry, charioteers, and crossbowmen. The first bladed weapons were made of bronze, which produced sharper blades than iron. The Chinese invented the crossbow before 450 B.C.E. to fire short, heavy arrows. The crossbow made chariots outdated, because archers did not need to get so close to the enemy. The infantry carried halberds. These shafted blades were fixed to long bamboo poles, so they could be swung from a safe distance.

TECHNICAL SPECS

- Sun Tzu wrote *The Art of War* in the sixth century B.C.E. It was the world's first military handbook and its strategies are still used today.
- During the Battle of Changping in 260 B.C.E., more than half a million men were killed.
- Hand-to-hand combat was the most common type of fighting in Chinese battles. Most soldiers used axes or halberds.
- During the Shang dynasty (c.1600–1046 B.C.E.), armor was made from bamboo and wood and padded with cloth.
- The introduction of iron weapons from the sixth century B.C.E. meant armor had to be tougher.

The crossbow

The crossbow was lightweight and accurate. It could only be developed thanks to advances in metal production. The bolt was released by a trigger pulled like that of a modern rifle.

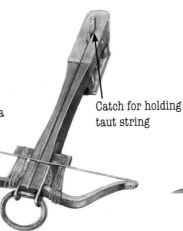

Catch for holding taut string

Trigger for firing

GUNPOWDER

One of the most popular ways the Chinese used gunpowder was to make fireworks.

Gunpowder is a mixture of charcoal, sulfur, and saltpeter (potassium nitrate). Its exact date of invention is a mystery. It is thought to have been sometime between the 8th and 11th centuries. Chinese alchemists were trying to discover a potion to prolong life. Instead, they caused an explosion.

The first reference to gunpowder was in 1044. The formula was called the "fire drug." The mixture burned and produced gases that expanded. If they were in a sealed container, it exploded. If gunpowder was put in a tube that was open at one end, the hot gas shot out a ball. These were the first firearms.

FIREWORKS

Gunpowder was later used to make fireworks. By adding different colored chemicals, the fireworks exploded into different colors.

TECHNICAL SPECS

- Fireworks were originally used to frighten the enemy.
- Iron or steel dust was added to give fireworks a sparkling tail.
- Bombs filled with gunpowder were launched from catapults.
- Rockets were filled with gunpowder that was ignited to shoot arrows.
- In 1220 c.e. the Chinese made bombs with outer casings that shattered to produce shrapnel.
- The first gun dates from 1259 c.e., when pellets were fired from a bamboo tube.
- The Chinese gunpowder cannon dates from the 1280s.

The gunpowder weapons invented by the Chinese in the 1280s became the basis of European cannons.

POTTERY AND PORCELAIN

Pottery has been made in China for almost 15,000 years. Over that time, it changed from rough pots to fine porcelain. Craftsmen developed innovative techniques for making and decorating ceramics. Porcelain production reached its peak in the Ming dynasty (1368–1644 C.E.).

China has rich deposits of the clay and kaolin needed to make ceramics. With the necessary materials at hand, the Chinese took the raw products and made pots.

Chinese potters created sophisticated shapes. They were also famous for their complex decoration.

Porcelain-making is still a major industry in China; here a vase is painted by hand before being fired.

TECHNICAL SPECS

- The earliest pots were made from coiled clay.
- Ordinary clay pottery is fired at temperatures between 930–2100°F (500–1150°C). Porcelain is fired at the much higher temperature of 2335°F (1280°C).
- When kaolin is fired at a high temperature, its physical makeup changes, a process known as vitrification. The kaolin becomes translucent and water-resistant.
- At their peak, China's imperial potteries employed more than one million people and used 3,000 kilns.

Around 2000 B.C.E. the potter's wheel was invented. This allowed potters to make round vessels with thinner walls. The vessels were fired in kilns. The Chinese introduced small vents in the kiln to keep the temperature constant during the firing process.

INVENTION OF PORCELAIN

Around the seventh century C.E., Chinese potters learned how to make porcelain. Porcelain is made from a mixture of kaolin and a mineral, feldspar. Unlike pottery, porcelain is hard, very fine, and translucent. The Ming decorated their porcelain with blue and white patterns, and it became highly sought after in China and Europe.

TIMELINE

B.C.E.

c.6500	Rice is domesticated in China.
c.5000	The Yangshao culture emerges in China.
c.5000	The first pottery is produced.
c.4000	The Chinese make bronze from copper and tin.
c.3300	The Liangzhu culture becomes prominent.
c.3000	The Longshan culture is the last of China's stone-age cultures to emerge.
c.2950	The Chinese develop a lunar calendar.
c.2700	Silkworms are cultured on mulberry leaves.
c.2700	Doctors begin using acupuncture.
2697	Indian ink is invented.
c.2000	Chinese astronomers record a first sighting of a comet.
c.2000	The potter's wheel is invented.
c.2000	The blast furnace is used to extract iron
c.2000	The Xia culture becomes prominent at the start of China's bronze age.
c.1600	The Shang Dynasty rises to power on the North China Plain.
1361	Chinese astronomers record a solar eclipse.
c.1360	Mathematicians begin using a positional number system.
c.1150	Chinese workmen cast bronze bells.
c.1100	The Chinese use spinning to make thread.
1046	The Zhou Dynasty replaces the Shang.

c.1000	Scribes begin writing on bamboo or paper.
c.900	The first cast metal coins are made.
c.700	The Chinese begin to cast iron.
c.600	Iron is used to make better plows.
c.600	The harness is introduced to make horses more useful for work.
c.475	The Warring States period begins. It marks centuries of conflict between China's states.
c.400	The Chinese use counting rods for calculations.
221	Qin Shi Huangdi, the First Emperor, unifies China by defeating the individual kingdoms and founds the Qin Dynasty.
c.214	The main section of the Great Wall is completed.
c.210	Qin Shi Huangdi dies and is buried with a "terracotta army."
206	A revolt led by Liu Bang topples the Qin and begins the Han Dynasty. Han rule sees long-distance trade with Europe via the Silk Road.
c.105	Traditional date for the invention of paper in China.
c.100	Mathematicians begin using negative numbers.
C.E.	
100	The multitube seed drill is introduced to plant seeds in rows.
100	The wheelbarrow appears.
220	The Three Kingdoms period begins as China fragments.
265	The rise of the Jin Dynasty restores order to China.
271	Invention of the magnetic compass.
302	Metal stirrups are in use by this time.

GLOSSARY

alchemist An early scientist who combined chemistry with magic.

Buddhism A religion that originated in India in the sixth century B.C.E.

canal An artificial waterway.

cast To pour molten metal into a mold and allow it to harden.

decimal A counting system that uses base 10.

dynasty A series of rulers from the same family.

empire A large territory ruled by an emperor or empress.

harness Straps used to control a horse or strap it to machines.

hoe A tool with a blade on a pole used for weeding crops.

irrigation Diverting water to the soil for agriculture.

kiln An oven used to harden pottery or bake bricks.

lodestone A type of magnetic stone.

moldboard plow A type of plow that turns the earth.

observatory A building used to observe the stars and planets.

pagoda A tower used as a temple or memorial.

parasol An umbrella used to provide shade.

porcelain A type of fine, translucent pottery fired at high temperatures.

seed drill A device that makes a hole in the soil to drop a seed into.

Silk Road A system of overland trade routes that stretched from East Asia through Central Asia to the Mediterranean.

spillway A place where water can overflow.

supernova The explosion of a very large star.

woodblock A way of printing in which a design is carved into a piece of wood.

FURTHER INFORMATION

BOOKS

Dramer, Kim. *The Chinese* (Technology of the Ancients). Marshall Cavendish Children's Books, 2011.

Greenberger, Robert. *The Technology of Ancient China* (The Technology of the Ancient World). Rosen Publishing Group, 2006.

O'Neill, Joseph R. *The Great Wall of China* (Essential Events). Abdo Publishing Company, 2009.

Snedden, Robert. *Ancient China* (Technology in Times Past). Smart Apple Media, 2008.

Strapp, James. *Science and Technology* (Inside Ancient China). M.E. Sharpe, 2008.

Te, Ting-xing. *The Chinese Thought of It: Amazing Inventions and Innovations* (We Thought of It). Annick Press, 2009.

WEBSITES

library.thinkquest.org/23062/
Thinkquest guide to ancient Chinese technology.

www.sjsu.edu/faculty/watkins/ancientchina.htm
Guide to ancient Chinese technology by San José State University.

www.ducksters.com/history/china/inventions_technology.php
Ducksters' history-for-kids pages on ancient China.

Publisher's note to educators and parents: Our editors have carefully reviewed these websites to ensure that they are suitable for students. Many websites change frequently, however, and we cannot guarantee that a site's future contents will continue to meet our high standards of quality and educational value. Be advised that students should be closely supervised whenever they access the Internet.

INDEX